# A Raven's Tale

## A story of two ravens' relationship with humans

Jane and Patrick Budd

# Table of Contents

# Preface

This is a story based on the observations of all ravens and other birds on Catalina Island. The observations have been over a lifetime, but during the last thirteen years we have studied them daily. We have used some research from others to compare and understand their behavior. A lot is speculation, but with repetition of behavior, we believe it to be true.

We have enjoyed interacting with our fellow ravens very much. They have made us laugh and we have learned that they too have their own type of feelings.

Ravens are mischievous, tender to each other, have their little spats and defend their territory, with the scars to prove it.

The fights in the air and on the ground can be fierce. Ravens will pin down another on its back, with their talons/claws and peck with those strong pointed mandobills (bills/beaks).

They do have a system of hierarchy, with submissives and dominants among the males and females, mated pairs, bachelors, and bachelorettes.

We hope you enjoy this story from the raven's perspective, and the next time you see ravens, enjoy them.

We believe all living creatures on this earth are connected.


Jane and Patrick Budd (The Humans)

# Introduction

We are ravens that live on Santa Catalina Island. Our ancestors flew here thousands of years ago. The Native Americans, called Chumash, lived on the Channel Islands and revered us (the ravens). They thought we were their ancestors (we are not telling). They let us steal their food with no resistance. So, as you can see, we have a long-standing relationship with humans.

Now, humans are angry that we are noisy, pesky, steal their food, and get into their trash.

We do mate for life and have territorial friends and rivals. We will put up with certain ravens and sometimes share our food, but others we chase away.

We are submissive to some and jump quickly or fly away, mostly because we have already established who the dominant one is, and we know he will beat the feathers out of us.

We can fly in a few seconds, from Pebbly Beach to the Casino, or we can take a day trip down the coast, but mostly we hang out at a place called 'Three Palms', above the town. All the visitors stop there to take pictures of the Casino, town and harbor, and sometimes they take pictures of us.

The following is our account of the relationship with the humans we befriended.


Greedy and Joe (The Ravens).

# Greedy

We started noticing two humans with a dog in our territory every day. When they started coming twice a day, we thought we would hang out to see if they had food. Where there are humans, there is always food. Well sure enough, they started bringing cut up hot dogs. What a treat, especially when you have to turn over rocks and leaves to look for bugs, dig in the trash or eat carrion or whatever to survive. Speaking of carrion (road kill), there isn't much on Catalina Island where we are except maybe a squirrel or snake that gets run over. I found a dead gopher snake on the road one day. I picked it up and flew up in the air with it and dropped it to make sure it was dead. It was another easy meal.

At first they did not know which one of us was female and which one was male. The humans were deciding names and since one had raised a raven chick, whose name was Joe, that is what they called my mate. Calling me Greedy covered either sex and Joe or Jo could be either. I truly can be greedy when it comes to food; I can stuff a whole lot in my gullet and bill at one time.

Greedy drinking water from the pocket in the rock.

A short time after we started following their schedule, I injured my foot in a fight and my middle toe was bent up. Our human friends could now tell us apart, not only by our habits and preferences, but I happen to be the only raven flying around with a middle toe hanging down.

Later, I injured my back toe on the same foot in another fight. It bends in and Jane says I strut around like I have a high heel on, like some kind of diva.

During the first spring we were all together, they finally figured out that I was the female. In early April I disappeared for a month, during nesting time. We start making our nests in February and March after picking a good tree, gathering sticks, and anything that can be cushiony on the bottom of the nest for our eggs. We tear up car or golf cart covers very methodically into strips and love outdoor furniture cushions. They tear easily and make a super soft bed for our chicks.

It takes 21 days for the chicks to hatch. Sometimes I lay the eggs a day or two apart. I stay on the nest caring for the eggs the whole time. Joe brings me food, but sometimes he stays so I can stretch my wings and visit with Pat and Jane once or twice during that time. When the chicks hatch, we still stay close to protect them, but we are both busy feeding more mouths. We have diversion tactics when taking food to our chicks that have hatched. We fly toward our nesting area a little different each time, down and up and around and about, coming to the tree from different angles. They grow fast and are the same size as adult ravens in just two and a half months. There are lots of reasons our eggs or chicks don't survive, but when they do, our chicks drive us crazy. After they leave the nest, they chase us around in the air squawking obnoxiously loud, and when on the ground, they squawk and flap their wings vigorously. Of course, it's all about food. They think the louder they squawk and the more they flap, that they will get fed over and over, but I remember who got fed and who didn't.

Joe and I usually have two chicks every year, but two years, we ended up with none. Usually in July, the chicks start following us to Pat and Jane. I faithfully feed them, poking the food I save in my gullet down their pink mouths and throats. The inside of the mouth stays pinkish/red from one to three years. It can vary according to hierarchy when they mature and then it turns black in maturity.

When they are teenagers and know enough to survive, we chase them away. At first a gentle peck or scolding, but later we get really vicious and show we mean, "Get out and get on your own!" Occasionally a chick comes back to see if they can get a free meal. Joe usually chases them away.

We are usually around Three Palms, an area above the town where the visitors stop to take pictures of our beautiful Island, the Casino, town, and harbor. This is our territory and one of our favorite spots to hang out. Jane calls us with her "raven calls"; three caws and our names and c'mon guys. If we are not too far away to hear, we will come. She can see us flying right at her, then closer, putting our legs down and landing so gently on the fence.

We know if she has a Tupperware container, it's probably really good leftovers. We especially love nachos, pizza, and fried chicken. I will not eat deli turkey or chicken, but Joe does. Mostly, we get cut up hot dogs every day, which we never get tired of. Jane feeds us evenly. She puts one piece down and says 'Greedy' and then another in his spot and says 'Joe'. Sometimes I am anxious and jump over and grab his food. Joe usually lets me with no problem, because we hide and cache our food for later to share.

When Jane takes Jack the dog for a walk, I will jump up on the back of the golf cart so Pat can hand feed me. I have gotten to trust him pretty well. I can stuff a lot of hotdog pieces in my bill really fast when he feeds them to me one right after the other, it's great! If he doesn't feed me fast enough, I will put my claw up and scratch the air to tell him, faster!

If Jane brings good leftovers with cheese, I dig right in and eat a bunch, then I stuff my gullet and bill with as much as possible, so some rival ravens won't get it and fly off to cache it somewhere. I usually hide my food in the ground, making sure no other ravens are around to spy on my hiding place. They will steal it as soon as I leave. I dig a hole in the ground with my bill and place the food there, pushing the dirt back over and pulling grass up to cover it, and sometimes placing a rock on top to mark it. I never forget where it is and may come back in a few minutes and move it again. Other ravens cannot smell where I put it, so they must see me hide it. We don't care if Pat and Jane see us hide our food as they are no threat.

Occasionally Jane will bring an egg for each of us. Sometimes they are raw and sometimes they are hardboiled. I can sense when it is light that I must be extra gentle holding it in my bill. One day, Joe just grabbed a raw egg up and busted it, so he had to stay there and eat it. That time the yolk was on him!

On some days there are a lot of rival ravens at Three Palms, so we must share. We do a little disturbed cawing at each other, but we don't like fighting when there are many ravens around. What can you do when you are outnumbered?!

One year, the General showed up with his mate, Crooked Toe. We usually yield, since he is a big guy and has already proved his dominance over us. When ravens are trying to show dominance to another, we do our baggy pants (lower feathers), puffy head feathers and fluff our wings out to make ourselves bigger. We strut around doing a clicking sound, putting our heads low to our chest.

Joe and I seem to have an edge over the local ravens in our territory. They know Jane feeds us and will walk between us and them so they can't get our food. It doesn't always work though. One day a new arrival who seemed unafraid of Jane and Pat, started coming around every day. They called him Bandit because he was fast and started jumping right in there and grabbing our food. He would walk right up to her and beg. Jane would say catch and Bandit would catch the hot dog piece in midair and she would say 'good boy'. Well, we can't have anyone edging in on our great setup. Something had to be done. I started catching food in midair too and was getting pretty good, but that wasn't fixing the problem. The problem was Bandit had to go!

After about a week of this, Joe and I said enough and fiercely attacked Bandit. We had him on his back holding him down in the street. He was squawking and scream-ing caws. Joe and I were holding him down together. One was holding his talons and the other bill over bill, so he couldn't peck back. Jane ran toward the three of us yelling and we all flew off. The next day things were back to nor-mal and we never saw him again.

One year during nesting time, a pair of ravens in another territory made a nest where it was too obvious and had it torn apart. It could have been rival ravens, a red-tail hawk, or even the eagle that cruises around our area.

We respect the eagle and usually fly in the opposite di-rection or make ourselves small and unnoticed. There are those of us sometimes who are feeling brave or stupid, that fly around the eagle taunting it. We also have osprey that hunt in our territory. One day, Jane and Pat were driving past Lovers Cove and saw an osprey grab a fish from the water and land on the hillside above the road. They stopped to watch and saw two ravens bravely working at getting the fish. One was in front taunting and the other behind pulling at his tail feathers. He was not going to let these pesky ravens get his meal. They gave up before one got hurt.

Red-tail hawks are a different story, because they are the same size as we are. We can spot one far away and start chasing it while he is trying to circle to look for prey. He tries to ignore us, but there are usually at least two of us taunting him. He gets irritated and occasionally flips over trying to grab one of us with his talons. We are fast, but can be injured or killed, so we give up and he moves on.

As a mated pair, Joe and I roost together in a tree at night as it gets dark. We don't like flying at night or in dense fog where we can't see where we are going. The bachelors and bachelorettes usually roost together in groups in one area. Staying in a group, the vagrant ravens have a social partnership that benefits them in many ways. We pair off around three years old, but sometimes before then.

In 2017, we lost our privilege to have Jane and Pat all to ourselves. A young pair of ravens showed up at Three Palms. We had several bad fights with one or both. We established that we still were the dominant pair, but they were persistent and kept showing up every day. We still fight occasionally and they impatiently wait till we are done getting our fill. Jane and Pat decided to call them Mickey and Minnie. Mickey is very aggressive and Minnie is very timid and they also know their names. Mickey does not like to wait and will walk Joe away with his dominant stance. Joe and I are getting older and are more careful about fighting now. Sometimes walking away is better than flying, since they chase us in the air for a long time to try to keep us away. If you walk you can still maintain your dominant stance and dignity. Eventually they get bored and give up. Mickey lets Jane or Pat feed him by hand. He likes it when we are not there, so he can get special attention.

There is another pair that showed up the same year at Mt. Ada. Their names were Walter and Winnie. Walter got tame fairly fast and would come right up to the fence rail to feed. Winnie remained very timid. She always turned her head to her shoulder in a shy way. They built a nest in the same tree two years in a row and Jane and Pat were able to observe them from the road. The first year they had four chicks and the second year they had none. Winnie sat faithfully on the eggs and only left to chase away intruders, then quickly returned. Walter was a bit selfish with the food and kept stashing it without giving her any. She finally cawed a scold at him to bring her some. The time went past when the eggs should have hatched and Winnie continued to sit on the nest for several weeks past. Jane and Pat could see her turning the eggs , but finally she gave up and sadly abandoned the nest.

Jane feeding Mickey near Three Palms. The tree on the road in
the background has Mickey and Minnie's nest.

When a eucalyptus tree is in a prime location, overlooking a good area for ravens, as they want their view unobstructed. So as a group, they begin to slowly and methodically strip the bark and leaves off either a branch or a whole tree. The tree will die and they all have a great view.

We have many different body languages, but one we do is swipe our bill back and forth on whatever we are perched on. This shows aggression or that we are displeased with something going on. We also just do it to clean our bill after a messy meal or digging in the dirt to cache our food. Another thing we do that I love is holding bills together along with a little "er" sound. We sometimes hold the others bill in our bill. The closed bill is offense and the open bill is defense.

We lose our feathers gradually during spring and look pretty scruffy for a while. Jane still says I'm a pretty girl. When we have molted and gotten our full feathers back, they shine iridescent in the sun. Juvenile ravens have brownish feathers until they reach adulthood.

One of the tricks we like to do is hang by our bill upside down, hanging on to a really small branch that sways with our weight. It barely holds us, but that is the fun of it. Sometimes we hang on with one talon and have a stick or small branch of leaves, switching between our bill and other talon. Then we drop and fly away or do a repeat.

The year of 2020 was a strange year. In the spring, humans started covering their faces. There were not as many people on the island, so less trash for us to pick through. The summer was very busy, with lots of people in rental golf carts at Three Palms again. Pat and Jane were worried because they didn't see us all summer. One day in the fall, we saw Jane walking Jack at the dump and flew down to the truck to see Pat. It was nice to eat hotdogs again instead of the trash. The next day they came and they brought us each a raw egg. Joe ate his right away, but I hid mine in a mound of dirt. The day after, when they came back, I went to my hiding place and brought the egg over to show them. Unfortunately, some of the other dump ravens saw it and I had to fly away with it in my mouth. They chased me all over trying to get my egg. Another day, Jane showed us some chicken she brought for us. We followed them until they got to the end of the road, so the other ravens wouldn't see it and try to steal our food.

So now Jane and Pat have three pair to feed, but of course we come first and are the favorites. I think we have it pretty good living on beautiful Santa Catalina Island.

Walter and Winnie

# Joe

We share our territory with many rivals. They are rivals because food means survival. Ravens are scavengers, so we eat anything.

When Greedy and I are lucky enough to have Jane and Pat all to ourselves, we can hide our food farther away in all our favorite caching spots. The area ravens know Jane and Pat always bring food, so if they arrive while we are gone, Jane waits to feed us. Uncut palm trees make a great place to cache food. They also make great nesting areas. Where we cache depends on how many ravens are close by and how hungry we are.

When we are scavenging, we walk around looking for bugs, but trash is easy. All we have to do is tear or pick at the trash bags. Sometimes Greedy and I go downtown and dumpster dive for our meals, but we find the trash cans at Three Palms and Mt. Ada offer a great meal after the partiers have been there the night before. If the Styrofoam containers aren't thrown on the ground, we have a method of trash retrieval. Greedy and I stand on the metal poles on each side of the trash cans, then we lift the heavy lid with our bills and off with the lid. Now we can pick at the trash. When the trash lid is already off, I have another trick I use; I stand on the edge of the trash can, pulling the bag up with my bill and holding it with my talon. If I am interrupted or lose my grip, I have to start over. I am persistent and eventually pull the bag up and get what I want and fly off happily.

Greedy can hold a lot of food in her gullet and bill. When she flies away and is being chased, she caws and it sounds like she has a mouth full of mashed potatoes. The others try to get her to drop the food, but she never does. Greedy got her name because she is good with food. When Jane brings bread, she tears it into many pieces. Greedy then methodically picks them up with the top of her bill pointing toward her chest. She picks each piece up stacking them in her mouth, usually stabbing the last one with the sharp point of her bill. She does French fries the same way, but often puts them back down to rearrange them. The smaller ones go in first, that way she can stuff more in. It's all a matter of logic.

When Greedy and I met Jane and Pat, we were already a mated pair. They have known us thirteen years and calculate our age to be at least 15. We are getting older and as Greedy said, we are careful about our fights now. Greedy has psoriasis on her legs and has lost her little leg feathers. She walks like she is nine months pregnant, with a waddle, but she still has a lot of spunk.

Pat feeding Joe on the back of their golf cart.

We interact with many variations of behavior, pretty much like humans. The young ravens like to walk around all puffed up and act tough, but we don't take them seriously. The easy way to discourage a submissive young raven, is edge up sideways clicking all puffed up with the dominant strut. They will usually jump or fly away. When we do have violent confrontations we can get injured. The worst ones are if a wing is sprained or broken. A sprained wing will hang down when we are perched, but will heal and we can still fly. A broken wing usually means doom for a raven. I injured one of my toes about the time Greedy injured hers. My inside right toe is shorter than the others, so Jane and Pat could pick me out in a lineup of ravens if they had to.

Hiding or caching our food for later is a priority. We will hide a few morsels first, then stop to eat. The days we are hungrier than others, we pig out as soon as we get our meal. We like to cache in soft dirt or trees, but can be very creative. The "town ravens" use house gutters and roof tiles, along with the usual tree.

If we are sitting perched on a stump or fence and see other ravens flying overhead, we turn our head to the side and look up with one eye and then turn to the other side and look up. This is usually when we are nervous that a raven will dive bomb us and try to knock us off. If they do attack, we usually hunch down with mouth open and squawk loudly.

A day at the dump, with the eagle and
some dump ravens on their favorite tree.

On hot days, we open our mouths to cool off. There is a large rock at Three Palms with a pocket cavity on top of it. Jane put some water there a couple of times for us to drink. Now if we need water, we will stand on the rock to let Jane know we want water.

We love flashy shiny things. One day I got silly and picked up an empty beer can with my bill in the opening. I flew around switching it from my talon to my bill. Jane was trying to follow my air acrobatics, when I decided to drop it next to her, to her great surprise. We do like to play and be mischievous. Sometimes when Jane is walking Jack their dog, we will swoop down over her head so she can feel the air move under our wings.

Some of the territories and raven neighbors we have are town ravens, Three Palms, Mt. Ada at Buena Vista Point, dump ravens, and of course the rest of the island. We all cross over territories at various times for food, adventure, and mourning. The food part is obvious, anytime, anywhere. Greedy and I have been seen at the Wastewater Treatment Facility or sewer plant as everyone calls it. We were with a gang feasting away at the waste (processed of course). When there is plenty of food, we don't fight.

Although I say we are rivals, many times dozens band together to fly and play in the wind. You will often see many of us flying circles way up above Southern California Edison Company, where there are warm currents. There are times when a fellow raven has died and we have our own kind of funeral. Dozens of us, even numbering 100, come from all over and fly circling above for hours, cawing frantically to mourn. We love windy days and will play "trust or dare" by flying together interlocking our feet with one another upside down and falling toward the ground till we break apart.

One day I came back from hiding some food in some dry grass. I landed on the stump next to Greedy. I realized I had a foxtail between my eyes, which was going to be difficult for me to remove. I turned to Greedy, telling her with a subtle little "er,er,er" to pull it out. She turned to me and gently pulled it out. Another day I was standing on the stump next to Greedy when a yellow jacket(bee) was bothering me. I think he smelled my hotdog breath. I snapped at it and swallowed it right up. I shook my head as I don't think he died right away. (Bzzz!)

We do like to sit with Pat and Jane after we have eaten and groom each other. The buzzard position, with humble body hunched down and head down to chest, shows we want to be groomed. We do a little low murmur in that position to let our mate know. We can be very tender to each other, gently moving our bill across and lifting a small area of feathers at a time. Of course we eat all things found. When I want to be groomed and Greedy ignores the signs, I scold her with a few low words of mine. She usually has a sassy remark back, but she's a female, so when she is not in the mood, I forget it.

One day a falcon flew near and a few of us flew off to chase him. After a few circles around, he got pretty irritated. He turned the chase around, pulled in his wings and dive bombed us. We took off fast, because he meant business.

Greedy and I recognize Jane and Pat whether they are in their golf cart or truck or even when they were in another golf cart some days. We will follow them up the hill, circling over, swooping in front and flying next to them. Sometimes Jane walks up the hill with their dog Jack, while we fly along following, lighting on trees as we go. We have walked with her up the hill also. If she doesn't notice us, we say one 'caw' to say, "Here we are." Then she talks to us and waves her arm and says, "C'mon guys." On days we show up late and see them going down the hill in the golf cart, we will fly across the front very close, back and forth to try to stop them. When they are in the truck, sometimes we will land on the street in front of them and jump, jump ahead to say "stop." They will stop to give us our daily meal and then we are happy. We don't like to fly past a certain point, because that is Walter and Winnie's territory.

We do spend some time just walking around picking up shiny papers or anything interesting, but mostly are looking for bugs under rocks or in grass. We eat small rocks to help with digestion. Ravens have a disgusting habit, but necessary, of regurgitating perfectly oval shaped pellets up. These are indigestible items such as egg shells, bones, and exoskeletons of insects, etc. The ravens that live in the interior of Catalina Island know that if they flip over a buffalo "chip" (feces), they will always find some good bugs living underneath.

One day, Jane and Pat were near their home and observed a town raven fly from a tree and attack a dove on the ground. He flew a short distance and started tearing it apart. Those that don't get fed regularly like we do, must do what they can to survive. It's tough, but it's nature in the raw.

Another day, Pat and Jane and Jack took a ride to the recycling center (better known as the dump). They were looking for the eagle that sometimes perches on the dead tree that is there. The pair of eagles were sitting there, just as majestic as can be, side by side facing opposite directions. Two of the dump ravens were above them on the tree also, sitting side by side. What a picture that was of the silhouette of those dried branches against the blue sky and those two eagles and our raven neighbors enjoying the day.

Mockingbirds are a pesky lot, especially around nesting time. The ones that also have Three Palms for their territory will not let up if we are somewhere near their nest. They will attack us on the head and will sit right next to us on the fence or utility line, just two feet away waiting for us to take off. They don't let up until we fly far enough away to their liking.

Our communication is much like humans. We use a combination of voice, body posture, and patterns of feathers. Ravens have quite a repertoire of vocalizations. Our talk sounds to humans mostly like a consistent string of 'caws'. Here are some of the frequently used communications. 'Gro' means friendship and is used for begging. Long raspy 'caaaws' are for intruders or we are disturbed about something. Low murmurs and soft 'oo oo's' are a relaxed state and content. Undulating 'quorks' mean "I'm here", rapped succession raspy 'caw caw's' mean "get away!" Gurgling is friendly. Rapid staccato calls are to predators, usually when we are chasing a red-tail hawk. We also make a sound like a succession of wine corks being drawn out of the bottle. We can go on sometimes "talking" with our rambling throaty warble. There are many more vocalizations that humans have a hard time figuring out, because they mean several things along with the body language.

Some body language examples are:

Jump up and back, jab unfamiliar objects with bill, then repeat and repeat. When near a rival, we snap our bills and walk with an assertive strut with bill held high. Male dominance is erect head feathers, bill snapping, bowing simultaneously with wings flared (our macho dance). Partially fluffed out feathers is a relaxed state, sometimes in combination with nictitating eye (white membrane moves forward to back over eye). Female knocking three times while bowing with fluffed feathers is a power display. (Greedy likes to do this a lot!)

For a while there was a raven with elephant legs and feet. They were gray not black and were three times bigger than our legs and feet. Jane called him Elephant bird. He had no feathers on his legs and his toes were very deformed. He had to fight harder for his food and was very aggressive. Jane felt sorry for him and always threw him a little food when he showed up. He was only around for a short while and never showed up again.

A few words about Jack the dog. He knows he is not supposed to bother us, but I can tell he just puts up with us. I am sure it is because we get special attention and some really good meals from Jane. Sometimes he will lunge toward one of us, but we know he can't get us. We watch with curiosity when he lets her touch him and pet his head. He must really trust her and get some really good meals from her too.

We love to fly around on windy days doing our aerial acrobatics. We fly with our mate or sometimes many of our friends in synchronized form. We will close our wings and do barrel rolls, dropping fast. Ravens are very agile in the air and can maneuver remarkably well. Sometimes we fly over Janes head so fast she can feel the wind in our wings and hear them 'whoosh'.

We didn't see our human friends for a few weeks. One day I was flying over the town and saw Jane at the truck.

The truck door was open, so I landed on it and looked inside. Jane said, "Joe, did you miss us?" She said Pat was in the hospital, but they would be up on the hill to see us soon.

As Greedy said, we enjoy being with our human friends. I think they understand us pretty well after all these years together.

# GREEDY and JOE

Ravens have been depicted as harbingers of evil and associated with death and doom throughout history. Therefore, many people are afraid when they see us. We get shooed, yelled at, and have things thrown at us. No wonder we are careful around humans. It took us a long time to trust Pat and Jane, but we still remember they are humans. Some days we are jumpier than others. We like sameness and routine, and prefer days that are quiet. On those days, after we have eaten or cached our food, we will talk with our friends in low tones and groom each other or preen our feathers while sitting next to them.

Well, that pretty much sums up our life with our human friends. Every day we look forward to seeing our friends, filling our stomachs, and flying off in the breeze. Now that we have gotten to know humans, they are not so bad after all.

IN MANY WAYS HUMANS ARE JUST LIKE RAVENS

# Raven Silliness

Greedy: I took a walk on the beach today.

Joe: Why?

Greedy: I wanted to make an impression.

Greedy: I went to the Silent Film Festival at the Casino today.

Joe: What did you think of it?

Greedy: I couldn't hear it.

Greedy: I dropped one right in the eighteenth hole at the golf course.

Joe: I didn't know you played golf.

Greedy: I don't.

Greedy: Know why they call me Greedy?

Joe: Because you can stuff so much food in your mouth at one time.

Greedy: Watch it mister!

Greedy: I'm wearing my scariest Halloween costume.

Joe: What is it?

Greedy: Nothing - humans are already afraid of us.

Greedy: I dropped a couple of white bombs at the mole (area where the boats load and unload passengers).

Joe: Why?

Greedy: Crowd control.